Wellbeing at Work

The keys to success,
health and happiness
in business

JULIUSZ WODZIANSKI

Acknowledgements

I would like to express my heartfelt gratitude to the many people who have helped directly, or indirectly, with this book, and in particular:

To Leda Sammarco who persuaded me that I had "something to say" and encouraged me to write and publish this book.

To Lou Beckerman, who has inspired me, and many others, with her selfless dedication to her work with sound and music with the elderly, ill and frail, and for her unfailing support.

To Ailsa McKillop who proof read the manuscript and helped me with the typing.

To Sharon Halls for her support and assistance with type setting.

To Marian Faulkner for her kind words and support.

To all of my work colleagues past and present without whom I would not have had the experiences on which to draw for this book.

And to Dr Craig Brown who kindly gave up his time to read, review, and provide a foreword for this book.

Table of Contents

Foreword

Many of the problems that patients consult for in general practice are related to stress at work. This may be due to a heavy workload, poor working conditions and difficult relationships with staff. The results for the individual can be anxiety and depression and for the employer days off with sickness and poor morale in the organisation. Turning to pills or alcohol is not the solution to this unhappiness. It requires a holistic approach that includes mind, body and spirit.

'Wellbeing at Work' addresses the issues in a practical way. Don't be put off by the word 'spiritual' because as the author, Juliusz Wodzianski', explains, it is simply stopping to give yourself time and space to look inwards to your own feelings and thoughts. You do have the inner wisdom to find the answers-if you slow down. This process, which is often called meditation, leads to a calmness and inner harmony.

The book is informative and structured in a way that makes for easy reading. You can quickly read through it then return to sections with the headings that interest you most. Part three: putting it into practice, looks at specific issues, and Part four some really helpful meditations. It is only with practice that you can really begin to gain the benefit from the meditations.

This book should be read by every employer in the country and be carried as a handbook by every employee. The result would be better working relationships and greater productivity. This is a manual in preventative medicine for healthy and happier patients.

Dr Craig Brown
West Sussex General Practitioner
Trustee of the British Holistic Medical Association.

Preface

My Background

I have worked as a lawyer for 22 years, in the field of commercial property development representing some of the most respected property development companies and institutions. During this time I have witnessed what is so common in corporations and organisations largely due, I believe, to not being true to what our souls require, but to the pursuit of profit often with scant regard to how we behave to achieve the aim of "success". That is not to say that some people involved in business are not spiritual, but very few will admit to having an interest in spirituality at work.

In addition to working as a lawyer I am a practising healer having been born with the "gift of healing", and which I have developed over time. Everybody has the ability to work with and develop their own healing ability.

I have been fascinated with spirituality since early childhood, and have explored many facets of this to date. As a child I read avidly about things to do with religion, with energy, with psychic phenomena.

As a teenager inexplicable things would happen around me. In my early twenties, I worked in various hospitals where people would often start to feel better simply by talking to me or being around me.

In my late twenties and early thirties, I concentrated on my legal career.

As time went on I recognised that by not fully embracing my spiritual interests I somehow did not feel complete and I felt that it was necessary for me to pursue it on a more formal basis. That formal exploration saw me undergo a healing course with the National Federation of Spiritual Healers (I was a vice president of that organisation for a time) and I underwent training as a Reiki healer (I am a Reiki Master / Teacher). My innate healing ability is, after all, part of who I am.

Undergoing healing training does not of itself turn anyone into a healer. It gives people a framework in which to explore and work with healing. Everybody has the ability to work with healing and develop this.

What is Spirituality?

I believe that spirituality is an important part of our being, and to deny this in any aspect of our lives is to deny part of ourselves. We are mind, body and spirit, and just as the body is more likely to have good health with exercise, a balanced diet, etc and the mind to be keen if stimulated, so the soul craves attention. And yet, it is the soul that is so often neglected.

Spirituality is the essence of life that runs through us but which cannot be seen, although it can often be felt if we are prepared to stop and listen. It is the quest and thirst for the understanding of life, and the purpose of life. It is the desire to know who and what we are, how we fit into the pattern of the universe, and what happens, if anything, after death. It is the desire for contentment, peace and understanding. It is the desire to understand how, if at all, everyone and everything is connected, and how it all works.

What Has Spirituality Got to Do With Work?

The amount of time that is spent at work generally forms the greatest part of one's waking life ie. it forms the major part of one's life. If we accept that part of the process of life is about seeking contentment, peace and happiness, then it must follow that we should be seeking these things in the workplace and not just in the evenings, at weekends and during holidays. In other words, we should all be looking to enjoy these things at every moment, in every place, in every way. Inner peace, contentment and happiness should be part of our everyday lives, at every moment, at work, in the evenings, at all times.

Sometimes it seems to be considered inappropriate to display the essence of spirituality in the workplace, which is not the way that things should be. There can be no incompatibility in your being what you are. We are all spiritual beings and we all crave spiritual upliftment and nourishment which can be provided in many ways eg. by listening to music, being by the sea, practising meditation or yoga, etc.

Furthermore, many companies are beginning to realise that the wellbeing of their staff and the economic wellbeing of the company are inextricably linked. I have carried out spirituality and healing seminars at

Essex County Council, BT and the Home Office (amongst other places). I will discuss these and their benefits in greater detail later.

The same principles apply whatever profession or work you may be involved in. There is no conflict in being what you believe in and carrying out your work responsibilities.

Feeling Stressed? You're Not Alone!

This was the headline of an article in the Law Society *Gazette*, (11 January 2007). The article reported that the number of lawyers seeking confidential help regarding stress, depression, alcoholism and other problems grew by more than 20% in 2006. A Law Society spokeswoman said: "We are extremely concerned about reports of solicitors being placed under potentially harmful levels of stress".

Out of the 424 helpline calls made to the charity providing support and advice to the legal profession some 67% were made by women. The chief executive of Law Care said "The bulk of these calls (around 67%) were made by women, who generally find it easier to share and talk about problems", and adds, "all firms and employers must manage the demands on their solicitors." It is to be hoped that in so doing help is being provided, and that some of the issues can be addressed and dealt with. What are the men doing, how are they dealing with the problems and or issues?

I suspect that this is the tip of the iceberg not only in law firms, but in many other professions.

The fact that people are suffering in this way is not only unacceptable in society, it is (for the reasons already discussed) unproductive, inefficient, and ignores totally the wellbeing of each individual, and by extension, the wellbeing of the workplace. How much sick leave is taken by people suffering from stress and / or depression, who cannot get up after a bout on the bottle? How many people go on to manifest physical symptoms and illnesses after prolonged stress and / or depression? How much is this costing employers in cash terms through lost productivity, locum and or temporary staff charges?

It seems to be the case that more and more professionals, at an early stage, are deciding that they are not prepared to put in the hours, to undergo the rigours and stresses of being a lawyer in a private practice in the City of London or other city, or other professional equivalent.

I think that it is a great shame that more is not done to promote spirituality in the workplace to ensure that people do not leave their chosen careers or jobs due to workplace unhappiness factors.

PART ONE: EMPLOYERS

Part One: Employers

Taking the Lead

As the boss, the direction of the organisation, the culture and the ethics follow your lead. The principles that are valued and rewarded, follow those that you value and reward. This is a big responsibility.

How many employers stop to consider this, and the major impact that their behaviour may have on the lives of many others?

We should also remember that this impact may well be a positive one which is both to be applauded and encouraged.

As a manager, director, partner or chief executive officer of an organisation you may take the view that it is necessary to focus on profit margins, product development, share prices and or other financial goals and criteria. After all, these are the benchmarks against which the organisation will be measured, and you in turn will be considered to succeed or fail on these performance measures. Whilst these things are important, if you engage in the workplace in a deeper way, not only can commercial success be achieved, but your company can become a more harmonious, highly functioning place, where people not only feel respected and valued but where they enjoy coming to work. So, you may be thinking "Just how can I engage in the workplace in a deeper way?"

There are a few basic principles that can be adopted based on spiritual truths that go a long way to ensuring that spirituality is present in the workplace. Things like honesty, integrity, respecting all, encouragement being shown, giving praise where praise is due, dealing with difficult decisions with compassion, allowing people to work with their strengths, help being given with weaknesses, giving and encouraging responsibility, all having a vested interest in the outcome. Listening and awareness are keys to many things. Honour the principles of honesty in communication. Starting out with the intention to treat all with respect is a very good place to start – I have seen many places where this has not been the case.

Over the years, some of my legal colleagues may well have thought that I cannot be a serious lawyer, what with being a healer, and being known to the public as such. It is interesting that my legal clients are aware of my healing practice and this does not give them any cause for concern. As a lawyer I am judged on the quality of my legal advice and deal making, not on the basis of my spiritual interests or practises.

Making a Difference

Engaging the principles of spirituality in the workplace will affect the business in a positive way if fully committed to by the leader of the business, and cascading from there. People who are motivated by feeling part of a venture, who are respected and encouraged, who are given responsibility and the opportunity to shine, will go the extra mile in seeking to achieve the goals that have been set.

Profit will increase, not decrease, absenteeism will be reduced, temporary staff bills will reduce. Treating people well is a mantra for success, whereas a drive for profit at the expense of people cannot succeed in the long term.

In addition there is nothing "new age" about the core principles of spirituality. They have been advocated by many through the ages of time as the teachings of many spiritual leaders show. We do not need to look far for such teaching as many of the religions of today are founded on them.

Increase Your Profit

Consider, for a moment, what is the cost of communication, what is the cost of listening, what is the cost of dealing with difficult decisions with compassion in a timely manner?

If you consider the time spent in listening, in embracing and promoting the welfare of all, as a cost unit, then yes, but this should be considered to be an investment in you and your staff, an investment that will repay itself many times over by way of increased productivity, increased profit, reduced staff turnover (who would want to leave a motivated, buzzing business?), reduced absenteeism.

Business is about the making of profit. Running a business with due regard to wellbeing and wellness, in an environment that nurtures all who walk and work in it, would surely help towards achieving profit.

If you see your physical body as a being that is to be driven solely in a manner that will produce the most physical output without any regard to how it is looked after, without any nurturing, with inadequate sleep, with no exercise, with not enough food and water, for how long will it be able to work in an optimum manner to bring about the best results?

Any business is only as effective and productive as each individual within it. By treating each individual well the business as a whole will thrive.

The Bottom Line

If people in positions of authority will not accept that for a business to be successful due regard has to be given to the principles of spirituality, there is a limited amount that can be achieved within the framework of that particular company for as long as that attitude is the one that prevails. It is often the case that the identity of the business and attitudes follow those at the top. (Remember that those that seek success will seek to emulate those in authority for their own career progression).

There are choices that each person as an individual can make, and we should not underestimate the power that we each have to effect change, and to make a difference by how we each behave at work and elsewhere. For some of us it may be that we wish to make such a difference as we can within a particular environment by living in accordance with our own principles of spirituality. In this instance employers may find that by listening to such employees and adopting their ideas in the workplace significant benefits can be had.

Others may choose to leave a particular environment to seek to work within one that they feel is more in keeping with their own ideals, whether with another employer or within their own new business set up. For the employer this may be costly for not only will talented people be lost (and recruitment costs be involved), but clients and / or orders may also follow the individual who has left.

How long can a business continue to be profitable if all you have is illness, and a business that is cracking under the strain of illness and unhappiness? For how long will a business survive with constant staff turnover? For how long will staff be prepared to endure long hours, a demotivated atmosphere and iniquities on the basis that they receive large salaries? Is money of itself enough to feed motivation and to keep loyalty, or does loyalty then belong to the business that pays the greatest salary? Is the irony of all this that in everything coming down to the bottom line staff believe that their return should also be solely in terms of money? Where does this all lead to, who benefits, who is truly happy in this circle?

Fun at Work

Business is about making a profit, but in a way that is responsible, and where people take responsibility for themselves, and their tasks. Work is a large part of life, and as such businesses and employers have major responsibilities to the staff that they employ, and the staff have major responsibilities to their employers. This is a two way process where one cannot smoothly function without the other, and yet so often it would seem that employers and staff are singing from completely different songbooks. Staff need to do their work to the best of their abilities, employers need to allow the staff to discharge this duty in the best way possible. Staff need to tell the employers if there are problem areas, if duties could more efficiently be done in another way. Employers need to listen, to allow change to be made to accommodate greater efficiency, to allow staff to fully engage in the responsibility they are showing and creating.

To embrace spirituality in the workplace is not necessarily the same thing as having constant fun at work, but how much better would it be if staff and employers engaged in their respective duties, had fun, had laughter, and sought to move towards that aim?

The key to all business is people and their inter-relationships. Where there is happiness and fun relationships are enhanced, business bonds become stronger, more work and / or orders are secured going into the future.

In one of my previous firms morale in the department in which I worked was poor. People were stressed, unhappy, and demotivated at work. I decided to take this up with the other partners in my department to seek to bring about some change in the way that things were run. The head of the department openly said that he did not enjoy work and that the only reason that he did it was to maintain his lifestyle as there was no other way that he could do this. We debated the issues, and I was told that as I was the only person who seemed to sense any of this, I was clearly wrong. The fact that I may have been the only partner that could see what was going on most certainly did not make me wrong.

Things went from bad to worse. One of the solicitors in the department went on long term sick leave, another resigned as she could no longer stand the atmosphere and the way that she was treated, and I told the head of my department that I could no longer accept his management. Another solicitor left. The senior partner became involved, and discussions were held. It was acknowledged that a problem existed, and the head of the department stated that he had committed to change, and which assurances were accepted by the partnership. I decided that the particular firm could not embrace the changes needed to bring it into line with what was necessary to accord with my ideas of spirituality in the workplace, even though a number of partners privately indicated to me that I had brilliant ideas, was innovative, and had the trust of the staff and assistants. I left that firm to take up a partnership elsewhere.

In another of my previous firms, I was troubled by the atmosphere in my department and the example set by the majority of the partners. After I had some time observing the behavioural patterns, I decided that enough was enough and wrote a paper called Success in the Workplace, which I circulated to the partners in my department and requested that this form the agenda for one of the regular monthly meetings. In brief the paper discussed my principles of spirituality in the workplace encompassing motivation, communication, respect, compassion, etc.

The meeting was duly held, and the paper was presented by me, and was discussed. To this day I can remember the exact words of one of the partners: "We agree with everything that you say, we just do not know what to do".

For me what this meant was that the relevant partners were not prepared to look at themselves and make necessary changes to how they were, and how they related to others. The best word to describe the reaction was one of "fear". Time and time again I think that fear is the constant thing that holds people back both on the personal level, and in business on a collective level.

Things remained the same, and again I decided that it was time for me to move on.

The Root of All Problems

Too often in the workplace those that are responsible for management lose sight of what is necessary or important to the people employed. This can be for a number of reasons including ego, corporate politics, and most damaging of all fear. The effect of this or a combination of them can be to focus inwards in a destructive spiral leading to degenerating morale, and the prevalence of negative energy.

Being united in fear never brings success, but often leads to the loss of people, work, and health.

It is also true to say that attitudes within the business environment generally follow from the top, so that a business leader who is energetic and motivated, who motivates others, who respects all that work within the industry, who deals with all fairly and compassionately, will create a motivated happy working environment. The converse is also true.

Valuing Your Staff

I happened to be in Pret A Manger yesterday and saw an advert for staff posted on the plate glass window: "We pay our hardworking, wonderful staff as much as we can afford rather than as little as we can get away with" was part of the advert, not as the "strap line" but as part of the copy.

This wording appealed to me, as it seems so right, that an employer should take this approach to salary. In the case of Pret, I do not how far this wording reflects the actuality, but the rates of pay were also set out in the advert, so no surprises on that score either. I must say too that the staff at this particular branch of Pret are always smiling and nothing seems to be too much trouble for them.

This has also been an attitude that I have found prevalent with the "partners" (staff) at John Lewis Partnership, where staff are partners in the business, and have a stake in the profits of the company. Not only that but I have found the service to be first class, and they have successfully traded on the "never knowingly undersold" statement for many years. Listening to the business news on Radio 4 this morning I heard that the profits for the John Lewis Partnership for the last trading year were expected to be very healthy.

In my own firm, salaries are at the top end of the range for our type of business, and the firm has invested heavily in people and resources to grow the business, and to take the business forward. Inevitably this impacts on the profit bottom line and the take home pay of the owners of the business, but the view has been taken by the partners that it is right to invest for the future, to leave a healthy business for those that are coming up through the ranks with the desire and energy to take things forward. It is also hoped that after an initial period the investment will produce returns.

So many firms, particularly where the major owners are nearing retirement age, decide not to invest in the future and seek to maximise the monies that can be taken out, with the result that premises become run down, the working environment becomes shabby, the monies available for distribution in salaries become smaller as the major owners seek to share the major profit between themselves. I have seen this happening in a number of firms and the end result is nearly always the same – staff leave, talented junior partners move to other firms taking their skills and loyal clients with them, firms become run down and either close, or a coup is mounted and there is bloodshed (not literally, although sometimes it seems as if it might lead to this) as the battle for control takes over.

In our commercial, materialistic culture, money and salary are fairly key factors, and financial and career aspirations (or a combination of them) are important issues for many people. Being paid well, and having enough money to meet bills and have the quality of life that one may reasonably expect to have are one of the main reasons that people work. There are clearly other reasons such as vocational work, being passionate about issues, making a difference in some way, having a structured meaningful day, academic interests, etc.

The bottom line though is that salary or wage levels are often taken to be a measure of a person's perceived value to the particular business or employer, and this in turn may well impact upon the person's own sense of self worth and confidence. It goes without saying that if staff are paid "as little as we can get away with" the quality of the input from staff may be as little as they can get away with. If on the other hand "hardworking, wonderful staff are paid as much as we can afford", this shows that the staff are important, are valued, are key to the operation, and are likely to respond in this manner. It is interesting too, to look at the structure of the sentence in terms of reference to "hardworking, wonderful staff". This, by its very definition is setting the scene that staff are expected to work hard, they are expected to be wonderful, this is the aspiration, the expectation, and they will be rewarded for these things.

The other logical conclusion of this wording is that the more profit that is made (as with John Lewis Partnership) the greater the financial reward that is available for distribution. Having a stake in the wellbeing of the business becomes having a stake on a personal level. As a collective whole, if all the staff employ ethical principles in their approach, the personal stake becomes a collective stake, one that takes on an energy all of its own and which potential customers and clients notice and react to. People are drawn to particular shops, professional advisers, etc, often without any conscious awareness of what it is that draws them, or why it, he or she or them feels right, or wrong.

Money, just like everything else, is energy, a commodity used for exchange and barter. There is nothing wrong with having money, or not having money. The only thing that matters is how you feel about where you are, about whether you are paid properly for the duties performed by you, whether you are paid on a fair and equal basis to others.

An organisation has to balance out what it can afford to pay in staff salaries and wages, having regard to its profit and loss account. It has to do so fairly, and openly. People who are sharing in business, who understand the position, who make choices in accordance with what is right for the business (which aligns with what is right for them on the basis that the health of the business means the continuance of their employment at a fair salary or wage) will be supportive of decisions made, why increases in salary cannot be made in a year when profits have fallen, where increases can be made in a year when profits have risen etc.

Some people say that there is no spirituality in money, that money is some form of bad or evil thing. This is not the case. Money is just that, money. It is an energy that can be used by people in whatever way they may choose. It is the choices made by people that influence how money may be perceived.

It's All About Respect

Respect is one of those things that has to be earned, it does not come with the title of boss, director, manager or partner. What does come with those things is the decision making process that will direct how the business, or parts of it, will be operated and run, and which will fundamentally affect the staff within the business.

Any boss who expects people to respect him or her on the basis that he or she is the boss, who tells people to do things because he or she says so, is likely to find that whilst things may well be done in accordance with the directions, there will be a lot of backbiting and gossip about him or her, and people are unlikely to go the extra mile in respect of seeking to complete the particular task or tasks expected of them. This sort of boss is essentially seeking to manage people through fear, through control of a negative sort, that is to say through fear that staff will be reported to a higher authority, that they will not receive a pay increase or a desired promotion, or fear that they may lose their job or be demoted.

Respect is gained through a number of different factors, and which will vary from person to person. Some of the key factors are:

Competence

Be accomplished in the field in which you operate, understand the processes, and be able and willing to step in and deal with any situation that may arise, coolly and calmly and bring about a resolution.

Keep up to date with the knowledge sector of the relevant profession or trade. Share your knowledge and teach the staff all that you know. Let the staff teach you what you may not know in so far as they have other or up to date knowledge.

Doing

Be prepared to step in and get your hands dirty when all are needed to be at the workface to accomplish a particular task on time, and to deliver the product. Be with the staff in terms of crisis, and in the good times.

Organised

Be on top of where things are, and what needs to be done. Arrange regular meetings with members of the team and ensure that the meeting timetable is adhered to.

Listening

Hear what staff are saying and give them a voice. Implement bright ideas that will move things forward in a positive way for the business.

Communication

Talk to the staff. Keep staff informed of work practices and changes and matters that affect them. Advise staff of achievements, orders won, new clients and the positive aspects of their business. Know the names of the staff (as far as possible – having regard to the size of some organisations). Greet the staff when you see them. Take time to "walk the floor" and see and ask how the staff are getting on.

Human

Be yourself, what you are, and communicate with all as you are, and not as you think you should be. Be confident that your skills are such that you do not need to hide behind an assumed persona. Do not be afraid to show your weaknesses at work, and ask for those that display strengths in those areas to work with you. Admit when you may have been wrong, thank staff for pointing out errors, for their ideas.

Delegation and responsibility

Delegate tasks to those that are able to take them on. Encourage staff to broaden their respective areas of operations and to take an interest in other sectors. Give responsibility to those who are ready for that and allow them the room to exercise that responsibility without constant meddling, but on the basis that there is feedback and regular communication. Do not use delegation as a means of handing over the problem matters that you do not want to be involved in or with.

Gratitude

Be the first to praise staff for tasks that have been done well, for things that are achieved, for having satisfied clients in their dealings, for having met targets, for their efforts and for having gone the extra mile. Celebrate achievements.

Dealing with difficulties

Where expectations and or tasks are not met or carried out, or there are perceived deficiencies in performance and or quality standards, promptly seek to discuss the areas with the relevant person or people (not in open forum). Seek to establish whether there are personal difficulties particularly if this is a new pattern, and or other things temporarily affecting performance (this does not mean that you need to go into detailed personal matters). If help is needed, or training issues arise, see if those things can be provided. Always seek to be constructive, have dialogue, be open to ways forward. If there are employment issues that arise deal with these promptly alongside the human resources team.

What is often overlooked in the business context is that business is about people, not money.

Productivity and profit are the goals of business, but these can only be achieved by person to person skills, not accountancy driven targets. Give a person a financial target in isolation and it is meaningless. Give the same person a motivated business environment where they are valued, their work and skills are valued, and watch the productivity grow.

Encompassing compassion and empathy in the workplace does not mean difficult things are not said, or dealt with. The difference is that things are dealt with in a timely manner and what is said is from the point of the heart and where the intention is a constructive dialogue and outcome.

Prove It

"Sickness absence is extremely costly for business, averaging eight days and £600 per employee each year. To tackle this, many employers are using high-tech methods to monitor patterns of sickness and identify problem areas. But experts say that nothing beats simple communication with staff". (Mail on Sunday, 7 January 2007).

Communication is more successful, achieves more than any high-tech method. Why this should be a surprise to business is something that I find a little difficult to understand, as it is such an important and basic point, and at the foundation of all dealings between people of which business is just one facet.

Later in the same article there was a quotation from an employee in a small Manchester based company (with a workforce of 110, including 25 office staff): "We do not feel pressured to come into work when we are unwell, it is more about feeling valued and wanting to do your best for your team".

There we have a living, breathing example of how individual employees feel about letting their colleagues down, about the importance of feeling valued, about how people will go the extra mile when they are.

In the same article it is also suggested that employers should be measuring the wellbeing of their staff, their levels of interest in their work and how engaged they are with their organisation. This would seem to me to be sound practice if it were part of an ongoing wellbeing regime operating at all levels of the business and how to improve it.

The article was headed "Keep your staff fit – by talking". Yes, by talking, by communication, with respect, listening, motivating, teamwork, all pulling together, this is at the essence of what is needed in business.

Again, the message is, feeling comfortable. The provision of service, "love your customer", provide the customer with an environment where they feel right, where they trust the store, where they feel that if there is a problem it will be sorted out, where quality at a reasonable price can be assumed, where the staff have an interest in the place in which they work.

Inspire Your Staff

Most offices are built to a fairly standard specification, with neutral colour walls and furniture. Most shops are designed to catch the eye of the potential customer, but back of store areas are not.

Very few workplaces are designed, colour wise, to inspire, uplift, or motivate staff, and likewise very few employers will consider having artwork or other pieces around the office to lighten the mood or soften the feel. Lighting too is often harsh, fluorescent tubes, which do not give the natural quality of daylight (how often do we see people becoming depressed during the dark winter months).

It is well known that colour, lighting, environment, have a major impact on how we feel, on our mood, on how we react and create. Even a few flowers here and there can significantly improve the feel, and attitudes within a working environment.

How often do we see artwork and flowers and attractive colour schemes, soft lighting in office reception areas or other front of house areas, but not in the working areas? It is in the working areas where the productive work is carried out. Should these areas not also be designed to uplift, inspire and motivate?

Making a Difference

At the next team or departmental meeting ask for ideas from the employees as to how they would run the business, the things that they would like to see, where they think things are right, where things are wrong, what could be better, what would make positive differences, what would bring out the best in each person, what would be motivating, how they would like to own and manage sections of the business, what they would like to be responsible for and how. Listen to those ideas with an open mind, be prepared to acknowledge that there could be benefit in change, that perhaps you as the business owner or manager may not have all the answers, that moving towards dialogue may be of benefit.

Now I would not expect that everyone at the outset would be prepared to discuss things openly in this way, particularly if everything has been carried out in a dictatorial style up to now. But stick with it; if the workforce sees that this is a genuine move towards an open culture with a view to enhancing the work experience for all, openness will come, ideas will flow.

When the ideas flow, follow those that are sound, allow the responsibility that is asked for, give ownership to those who are wishing to take it, allow the business to flourish with and through the ideas of all participants.

Remember that without all of the people, in all of their respective positions, no matter what the duties, there would be no business. The single most important asset of any business is its people. Are they treated in the way that is consistent with this?

Be yourself, free of masks, and carry out every task and interact with everyone in the workplace with compassion integrity and honesty.

Ethical Principles in Practise for Employers

Unhappiness in the workplace can arise for many reasons, but there are issues that can be addressed by the management of any industry to create a more cohesive environment, to enable people to fulfil their potential and thereby increase productivity and profitability.

There are, in my view, five principles which if embraced by management and practised (paying lip service and leaving things to others is not practice) will raise the nature of energy in any working environment, as follows:

Professionalism

Treatment of all persons with respect and dignity. Recognition that everyone plays a critical part in any organisation and everyone is an important member of the team. Avoidance of personal comments that may be hurtful or demeaning. Carrying out of one's duties to the best of one's ability in accordance with all professional or trade requirements and in a quality manner. Fulfilment of clients' expectations. Dealing with all things promptly, in a timely manner, and finalising any discussion or matter started with due diligence.

Knowledge

Keeping abreast of developments and changes in the field, and sharing this information with others.

The recognition of one's (and others') own limitations and strengths. The institution and maintenance of quality control and training and information supply and drawdown. Efficient, timely and proper delegation and supervision.

Compassion

Working with others from the basis of care and understanding, and with a common goal. The proper treatment of all irrespective of personal differences whether in terms of ideals, religion, culture or simply not understanding. The uniform application of principles in the workplace to all without favouritism. The making and execution of difficult decisions in a correct and respectful way, and the communication of such issues in a proper and timely manner.

Nurture

The recognition of people's strengths and weaknesses and working with these different abilities to bring out the best, from all, as a team. Providing encouragement and reward for duties and matters carried out. The communication to individuals of the things expected of them, and the ideals of the business. Open discussion of all matters that are not confidential. Making all feel part of the team, and the bringing of loyalty through such treatment. Discussing career paths and patterns with individuals openly, and honestly.

Vision

The focus by the business on where it wishes to be, and putting in place the strategy to get there. Bringing all into the path of the ideals and practice, thereby generating enthusiasm on a collective level.

The practice of the principles of professionalism, knowledge, compassion, nurture and vision bring real and positive benefits. It brings communication, greater harmony, and most importantly of all positive energy. Businesses that are positive, energetic and enthusiastic and where people work as a team are usually successful. They are also terrific places in which to work, no matter what position is held.

Taking Care of Your Staff

I have always been concerned with the welfare of people, and as such I make a point of having a chat with everyone throughout the office on a regular, if not daily basis. I talk to everyone involved in the business. I sing happy birthday to people in my team. It is so clear to me that the input of everyone is key to a successful business, and business is about people.

The result of this is that people often confide in me in respect of issues that they may have relating to work, or sometimes those of a personal nature. Such confidences are respected at all times, and these things are never disclosed to other members of staff, or managers.

In a previous firm the partners sought to utilise my "people skills" in seeking to have me as some sort of unofficial confidante, which would have been fine, except that what some of the partners meant by that would be that I would somehow come into the control equation by effectively listening to the issues, and then reporting back on them, with names and details. The fact that I instinctively knew what the areas of difficulty were, and raised these with the partners of my own volition (but without back up from any individuals) was not relevant to them. It goes without saying that I could not operate as some form of stooge salvo, and so this attempt could not succeed.

Every business needs to have a forum at which, and by which, issues can be raised, and discussed, anonymously if necessary. This can be the human resources department, but often staff are fearful of raising issues in this way as they feel that what they say may go direct to the management. Others may appoint a manager or partner as the staff liaison partner, which is fine if this is a genuinely independent situation without an expectation that the relevant partner or manager is going to reveal all confidences to the rest of the management team, except where this has been discussed and agreed with the relevant individual.

More and more organisations are now using a counselling model of dealing with staff stress issues, often out of house, by which individuals can arrange for an appointment to talk through their issues or work problems with an independent professional who is bound to confidentiality under the code of conduct that he or she subscribes to.

How much better it would be if all people involved in the business were encouraged to be open and truthful in all their dealings in the workplace, if any issues could be discussed openly and without fear of recrimination or reprimand, and if all business could be conducted with a view to the welfare and wellbeing of all of the people involved in the business, and which in turn would lead to the welfare and wellbeing of the business.

It is no accident that businesses that are run by motivated, compassionate and passionate people with a clear vision and focus tend to be successful and happy places in which to work. It is no accident that John Lewis Partnership where all staff are partners in the business and share in the profits of the business, report strong results year on year in the rather unpredictable retail industry. The fact that John Lewis Partnership was set up on the basis of ownership by its staff was ahead of its time, and whilst not necessarily a model that others would wish to emulate, certainly gives food for thought, and a lot of the principles involved in the strategy can be considered as useful for other business models.

Communication, Communication, Communication

Having a forum in the workplace where a suitable and supportive environment is provided, where constructive and informative discussion can be held would be a helpful tool in encouraging communication. The forum could be facilitated initially by a professional (perhaps a human resources manager with the appropriate experience) to seek to ensure that the forum is used for open and constructive discussion rather than as the opportunity to whinge and gossip.

Being Allowed to be Who You Are

Individuals are not separated out from who or what they are when they leave home and come in to the workplace. Individuals still have their issues, beliefs, personalities, likes and dislikes whether they are at work or at home. People are at their best when they are allowed to be who and what they are.

It is time for employers to take note of this, for necessary changes to be made, for employers to be in the vanguard through their leadership and example to embrace spiritual principles in the workplace, for this to be the norm and the expectation within the corporate culture of the business.

Wellbeing Days in Organisations

Some organisations now arrange for a facility whereby staff can book sessions from a therapist (whether on site massage, reflexology, shiatsu, Indian head massage, or other) during the working week, in the office, often at the cost of the organisation. Those organisations that have provided such benefits generally find that far from productivity being reduced following a session, it is actually enhanced.

There sometimes seems to be a misapprehension that being relaxed means that the ability to concentrate is reduced. This is not how it works. Being relaxed means that the whole of the being is more open to ideas, less cluttered, more able to fine tune and focus.

There are good business reasons to consider the provision of therapists within the workplace. And the staff will appreciate it too!

I set out below case studies in respect of some of the wellbeing days I have been involved with:

Essex County Council

I have been involved with staff conferences at Essex County Council for two years running.

These consisted of a number of activities from which Essex County Council staff could choose. With those in my group I began by discussing principles of spirituality in the workplace, carried out a guided meditation, and then gave individual healing sessions to each member of the group.

Juliusz's presence had a calming effect on everyone. Even though we are all striving to succeed in a stressful world, he gave us a fascinating glimpse into how to remain healthy, happy and at peace with ourselves (2004 staff conference).

...your sessions were again well received. Staff commented on how relaxed they felt and how calming your voice is. They also noted that the atmosphere in the room was very spiritual (2005 Work / Life Balance Day)

BT plc

I was a keynote speaker at the first wellbeing day at BT plc, where I gave presentations on stage discussing various aspects of wellbeing. I spoke about the principles of healing, and conducted a question and answer session, and gave demonstrations of healing (with participants drawn from the audience).

At the second wellbeing day I attended at BT plc, I gave individual healing sessions to staff members in the therapy area, and in the afternoon, I conducted a guided meditation on stage for the audience.

Juliusz W's skills and energy captivated and relaxed his audience in a matter of minutes. He got them focused with his magnetic voice and choice of words. The delegates left saying they felt at peace and in a calm state of mind – great way to have ended our day.

Home Office

At the Home Office wellbeing day I was one of two "therapists" who were involved, the other being a sound therapist. I gave individual healing sessions to Home Office staff. All those who received healing, many for the first time, were amazed by how relaxed they felt during and after the session.

Conclusion

Having read through Part One of this book you might be thinking that being an employer is a big responsibility. Perhaps consideration had not been given to the impact that his or her decisions and attitude would have on many other people. All too often being a manager, or a boss, is considered by an individual as a personal career step rather than as a position of responsibility for the wellbeing of others.

Being an employer brings responsibility, but the potential for bringing about positive change and growth is also there.

By discharging the responsibilities of an employer to nurture wellbeing in the workplace, the employees benefit too. Everyone benefits.

PART TWO: EMPLOYEES

Part Two: Employees

It's Not Just Top-Down

In Part One of this book we have looked at how employers influence the workplace, and how their behaviour has a major impact on the culture within the working environment. Employers are one aspect of the whole workplace equation. We now need to look at employees and how their actions can influence the working environment and what individuals can do to help themselves in the workplace.

Taking Responsibility / You Have The Power/ Create Your Reality

Thought is very powerful and all things follow thought. An individual can influence what happens in their own lives by creating, holding, and believing in an idea. And whatever an individual can create on an individual basis can be multiplied a hundredfold when the collective thoughts of an entire business, or a significant proportion within it are working towards a shared vision. As with all things thoughts and shared visions can be positive, neutral or negative.

If a business is negative, so it can change with the collective thought input of those involved in the business. This is the process of creation that occurs on an individual and collective basis. The process of my writing right now is not an accident, it is my creation to enable others to manifest their own creation to the place that they wish to be in.

Be creative, create your reality – you already do so, so take control and create the reality that you wish for.

Good Boss, Bad Boss

If it is the case that management is poor, that people are not looked after, if personnel management skills are lacking, if spiritual principles are not heeded in the workplace, then as indicated elsewhere in this book it is highly likely that there will be problems in the workplace as attitudes tend to flow down from the top, from the vision that is created or in place at the firm. Vision can be a negative one or the lack of one in this context.

However not all problems stem from management. It is possible that the management do their best to comply with spiritual principles in the workplace and to create a good and pleasant environment in which to work, but somehow this does not translate into a happy working environment. If the employees are not interested in improving the workplace there is very little the management can actually do to make this happen.

You too are responsible for the working environment, this is not a one way process whereby the management are responsible wholly for your welfare, happiness and wellbeing. You are entirely responsible for yourself and how you conduct yourself, how you react to others, and for practising spiritual principles in your conduct and dealing with others. This is not something that you can leave to others, or that others can deal with. In other words, be and live the change you want to see in the workplace.

If the management are striving to produce the best working environment possible in the circumstances of the business, and every effort is undermined by staff complaining and gossiping and failing to take responsibility for themselves and their areas of practice, and failing to raise their own personal game to seek to achieve change for the better, then this is just as bad as management not listening. Whilst this is not likely to happen in practice it is worth mentioning by way of highlighting the point that the business relationship is dependent on co-operation and everyone playing their respective parts.

So the process of change is a two way, or more, thing. Managers need to be prepared to listen, adapt and change. Staff need to be prepared to listen, adapt and change. Managers and staff need to talk together to enable this to happen, to move with the times, move with trends and business flows, to be able to react quickly to changes in the business environment.

Staff need to input their ideas as to the best way to achieve their tasks. If the decision is that the ideas are sound, the staff should have responsibility to implement the ideas and take responsibility for those sections.

So often the feeling in business is that there is the "them and us", the bosses and the staff. No, the success or failure of any business depends on the collective will of all involved in the process, everyone plays a crucial role in the smooth running and operation.

In a previous firm I recognised that staff were de-motivated, across the board. By talking to those that I worked with, encouraging them, thanking them for a job well done, by celebrating completed deals and by standing up for them when they were unfairly challenged I took steps to seek to increase happiness, to encourage the taking of responsibility, to individually perform as well as could be and to take pride and happiness in what was happening. This worked well for my own secretary who was very happy working with me, and various members of the office staff were very responsive to my efforts.

However many others did not want to seek to embrace change, or do anything about their unhappiness, they seemed to be happier in their state of unhappiness making destructive comments about others, complaining about how awful it was at work, living for the weekend. I make no comment as to how anyone should live their lives, and what they should do on an individual basis. It is clear though that the only way that people can be happy is by seeking to change for the better, by adapting and by taking responsibility. Sometimes this can be about changing views and attitudes built up over many years. This can be done, and if it is, the rewards individually and collectively are immense.

Only you can change aspects of yourself to help to increase your own wellbeing and happiness.

How to Succeed

Interviews

Just as you are being interviewed by the organisation, you are interviewing the organisation. Do you want to work within this particular environment, do you feel that you can work alongside the prospective boss, how does the culture feel to you, is this organisation right for your skills, will the position and organisation suit your curriculum vitae? Listen to what your intuition tells you about this place – do you feel comfortable and at ease, or do you have a feeling on unease or discomfort? Does the environment feel right, do the people that you have met treat you in the way that you would expect to be treated, do they seem happy and engaged in their work? Do you feel that you will be comfortable spending many hours each day with these people around you?

An interview is a two way process. So many people going for interviews feel that they are being put on the spot, that it is some form of unpleasant cross examination. Naturally the organisation will want to know about you, your skills and abilities, how you react under pressure, but these are work related qualities that do not go to the heart of how worthwhile and wonderful you are as a person (which you are).

Remember too that you are being interviewed by a person, or people, who are on their own journeys in life, who have their own issues, challenges, concerns and worries, and most importantly who are human with all the frailties and emotions that come with that. The interviewer, or interviewers, may be more nervous than you are (even though they may have more experience of interviews than you).

A well conducted interview should be a fact finding session, a two way process of discussion and exploration, a respectful and courteous exchange of information and ideas.

If you are in a situation with an interviewer who may be aggressive or difficult, bear in mind that this may well be their way of dealing with their own insecurities, the mask that they wear to cover what they consider at a deep level to be parts of their personality that they do not feel that they can reveal for whatever reason. The same will be true of any boss, or other person that you may come across, in whatever walk of life that displays these tendencies.

Before going to an interview, take time to find your own place of calm and peace, seek to retain your equilibrium during the interview, and be yourself.

Be yourself, be true to yourself, you would only wish to be in an organisation where you can be yourself and work as a respected member from that place of truth.

Being Promoted

If you want promotion then you are likely to be granted your wish and to continue to want it.

Earlier I mentioned that thoughts are very powerful energy emanations that are sent out to the universe, and have the effect of creating a course of events, and that the resultant effect will often be a manifestation of the thoughts in reality. In other words, you create your own reality, every minute of every day, with every thought, the energy that you put out, and the energy that is attracted back to you, is in accord with what you are putting out.

So if you want, then you will continue to want, and so it goes on, round and round in circles.

Remember too that there is no past or future in the present, there is only the now, this moment in which you are living, this moment when you are reading these words. To wish for something in the future too, is also going to lead to something never landing, it will always be in the future, never now.

To create the ability to have the promotion that you may desire, or whatever else may be your wish for part of your life, and which you wish to create, it is necessary for you to see yourself as being in that place now, doing, being, having those things that you wish for. Not a throwaway "I wish that I had that", but a heartfelt belief and focus on the subject of your wishes, continuously without falter or failing.

For your desired promotion, act as if you had already been promoted. Take on the responsibility that goes with the promotion, do the job to the best of your ability, beyond the expectations for your level or grade, communicate with your clients, customers, colleagues with confidence, in accordance with the principles of spirituality in the workplace.

Respond to the managers or partners with confidence, promptly, surpassing their expectations. Take responsibility for yourself, your work tasks, help others within your team or group where you are able to, be generous with your time and knowledge.

By living and acting as a person who has been promoted, you will be promoted or headhunted.

The ability to create and manifest your destiny, the creation of your reality, is a very real and ongoing constant process, in constant flux and change. If you are steadfast in what your focus is, your focus will manifest in reality. If you give off constantly mixed messages, if you cannot decide what you wish for, if you keep changing your mind, then that is what will come back to be your reality i.e. indecision and uncertainty and things being neither one thing nor another.

There is a saying that goes something like "be careful what you wish for, it may just come true".

I am good at my job but it is always one of my colleagues who is promoted. Why?

Some organisations have criteria that are laid down as to what benchmarks need to be in place, met or passed, for people to be considered for promotion to the next stage in their career path. These targets can be fee targets, recorded time targets, sales targets, practice development issues, man management skills together with what sometimes seems a plethora of additional matters. For those that stop to think on the subject it does not escape attention that often those who are currently in positions of management might well not meet the relevant criteria that have been imposed as competition becomes stiffer, as the numbers seeking promotion become greater, as the number of managerial positions become lesser.

Where there are a number of candidates who are to be considered who have all satisfied the criteria for promotion, there can be little complaint as to the fairness of the selection and or process, even though it may be difficult for the unsuccessful candidates. What is hoped for in these circumstances is that the unsuccessful candidates will, in accordance with the principles of spirituality in the workplace, continue to work closely as part of the team and be supportive of the newly promoted person, and that the newly promoted person will welcome the support and encourage the others to work towards their own personal goals.

What is rather more difficult is the situation where the candidate who is selected has not met the criteria that have been set in one or more categories, but a blind eye has been turned towards the point or points in question on the basis that there may be "exceptional circumstances" and which is usually a code name for "favouritism" It may well be the case that the particular individual is excellent, that the position is well deserved, that the business will be well served, but for those that have been unsuccessful this will send out a clear message that they have been passed over on the basis of "someone's face fitting" rather than on the basis of achieving the criteria that have been set.

There may be many reasons for this happening, and no doubt a lot of this comes down to basic human principles and instincts of survival, and the like. Managers who may not be overly confident in their own abilities may well feel threatened by those who have qualifications and/or experience which exceed their own, people who feel more comfortable with people of a certain type may not wish to promote those that do not fit this section (irrespective of employment legislation), people may wish to seek to promote those that in some way will make the particular manager look good. There will be a whole range of reasons.

In a work environment which works within the context of spiritual principles none of the above would occur as everyone would be working together, all would be an integral part of the business, the function of one person would be regarded as hugely important, all would be valued, and hence "favouritism" could not, and would not, be part of the working process.

Whatever the position may be in your organisation, if you employ spiritual principles at all times at work, the right thing will come to you and for you, whether in that organisation, or another. Live and work in the now, and be aware.

De-Stress At Work

There are a few techniques that I use in the office if I begin to feel stressed, or under too much pressure. In some ways it is reasonably easy for me as I have worked with meditation over many years, and so I can go into a calm place wherever I may be. This is a technique that has been of invaluable help to me over the years. Sometimes very easy, straightforward things can make quite a big difference to how you may feel. I set out some suggestions below:

Take a few minutes out when you make yourself a cup of tea, when you visit the toilet, when you take a break for lunch.

In those times when you are stressed and you cannot leave your desk you can (without anyone noticing) sit at your desk take a few deep breaths, allowing the energy of the life force to be taken deep into your lungs and circulate around the whole of your being bringing instant healing and replenishment.

If you go outside at lunch time you can take in the green of the leaves on the trees, the green of the grass or the foliage within any window boxes or office foliage displays.

You can put your hands on your tummy allowing healing to circulate from your hands around your being.

If you have a headache you can gently run the tips of your fingers around the temples of your forehead for a few seconds to help to lift this.

In the being that is your body you can envisage and create your own healing systems and methods that you can employ anywhere, whether in the office, on the tube, walking to work, or watching television.

PART THREE: PUTTING IT INTO PRACTISE

Part Three:
Putting It into Practise

Challenges

The outward manifestation of spirituality in the workplace is the display of core attitudes that enable all to work in an atmosphere of respect, where people are rewarded for their input, where staff progress on merit, where favouritism is not shown, where bosses listen to staff, staff listen to bosses, where dishonesty and laziness are dealt with robustly but with compassion.

It may seem that dealing with workplace issues is too complex an area to seek to resolve, that there are too many competing stresses and strains working against each other to allow wellbeing to manifest. It may seem far simpler to leave things as they are.

The challenges that are faced in the workplace are those that both employers and employees are subject to even if the issues sometimes appear different. An employee's problem if left unresolved will become a problem for the employer and the converse is also true. By the employer and the employee working together the solution can often be found to the issues and problems that manifest bringing about their resolution and helping to restore harmony in the workplace.

How to Release Stress

Releasing stress and tensions held within would be a good start, and would bring benefit to you, and to all in the workplace. The problem with this is that with our good old English stiff upper lip resolve, people are not willing to admit to, or discuss, their problems or innermost feelings for fear of being seen to be weak, or not able to cope.

People nowadays are without their extended families, the number of people living alone, or in small units, is increasing, and more and more people are living a life on a conveyor belt of stress, fast food, inadequate exercise and pressure. It is an irony that people become ill to make money, and then spend all their money seeking to regain their health. It is also the case that people may seek to deny that they are stressed, that they cannot cope, and of course many people will seek to deny that there is any truth to spirituality, or the concept of love or divine truth.

Just As You Are

The key to happiness in the workplace, and in life generally, is to treat others as each of us would ideally like to be treated. In essence this means treating all people with respect, listening to what others have to say and not rushing in to get our own point of view across and / or talking across another and treating everyone with compassion. Again honesty, integrity and communication are key elements to happiness.

Loving people in the workplace does not mean that any of us should wish to hug another, or even that we have to necessarily like everyone in the workplace. It means working together in a harmonious way with a common objective and vision pursuant to which the objectives of the business can flourish and each individual can feel motivated and fulfilled as part of a team.

Don't judge yourself, and stop trying to see yourself as you perceive others may see you. You will never be able to see how others may perceive you, and if you did you may well find that there is no resemblance between what you think, and what they perceive. The only reality that you have is that which you perceive, so what others may see or think, whilst being a useful sounding board, does not affect your reality unless you choose to make it so. All things result from your choices, your thoughts, what you create, what you attract on the basis of what thoughts you send out.

The second thing to do is to start to accept yourself as you are, to realise the truly wonderful being that you are, the beauty of your soul, that you were born as a perfect being to live life, to experience it to the full, to allow yourself to experience the wonders of divine nature and creation, part of which you create on an ongoing constant basis, with every thought.

Every thought that you have, that is sent out, will potentially create and manifest in reality.

Spend time with yourself, let out repressed emotions, anger and trauma, be honest with yourself and others, live life in the way that is right for you.

Communication

It is useful to remember that ideas, of themselves, of any person are not right or wrong. If implemented, some ideas may work and others may not. Most creativity in the workplace emanates from open discussion where ideas are freely exchanged and a new direction is taken based on a collective approach.

I do not see what I say as necessarily being right, but I can always see things that (to me) are wrong and against the principles of spirituality in the workplace. It is at this level that I see the fundamental problem in most workplaces that do not embrace spirituality, that is to say bosses being closed to problems and or denying their existence and / or refusing to acknowledge that anything could possibly be wrong in a business model that has been utilised since the business was first formed.

Right and wrong don't matter. What matters is the openness to the dialogue, to the creation, to the making of decisions and implementing the decisions made promptly and the giving of credit to those where credit may be due. Decisions too (made in accordance with the principles of spirituality) are neither right nor wrong. Some on implementation will appear to work, others will not. The beauty of this method of creation is that with constant and open dialogue and feedback things can be monitored, fine tuned, improved and changed on an ongoing basis.

Remember That Things Come Around

There are those that say "things that go around come around" and variations on the theme. Others believe that every action creates a reaction, and that every thought is energy that goes out to the universe and creates an effect.

There are those who think any principle that suggests that the activity of you in Britain can have an effect on others in Australia cannot be the case (even though it is!). Whatever an individual's own views on these matters may be, it is generally acknowledged that the world is a pretty small place, and is getting smaller all the time with increased ease of travel and communication and advances in technology. This is also the case with the legal world, and the specialisms within legal practice. We can be pretty sure that at some point or another we will come across people that we have dealt with previously, again, whether lawyers on the other side of transactions, people moving within client's organisations or whatever.

One example that I would give is that some years ago I was acting for a property development client who was forward funding an office development scheme (basically meaning that the freehold interest in the property was sold to a funding institution who then provided the finance to develop the site, and if the development went well, a profit to the developer). The person who was acting for the funding institution at that time was a junior lawyer within one of the major City of London firms of solicitors, and whilst very able, did not have much experience of these transactions. I went out of my way to structure the transaction to take on board all of the points that were appropriate to both sides, and to create a balanced transaction. (I have experienced situations where lawyers on the other side have done anything but!) The transaction went ahead, and everyone was satisfied with the outcome.

My client retained some land adjacent to the land that was sold to the funding institution that they were going to develop out after the first development had been completed, with their own resources. As they carried out the development the building contractor, unknown to the developer, carried out works on the land that had been sold to the funding institution some years previously. These works needed legal deeds to be entered into which had not been obtained.

The development was completed, let, and was due for sale when a very meticulous property project manager spotted the unauthorised works. This could have prevented the sale of a multi million pound development.

The lawyer who was junior at the time of the forward funding transaction was now a senior lawyer still acting for the funding institution, which still retained the interest in the land.

The funding institution, when approached for the necessary deeds to rectify the position, could quite easily have refused, or required a large sum of money for the grant of the rights.

The lawyer acting for the funding institution agreed to grant the necessary deeds on the basis that their costs were paid and no more. If I recall accurately the words used were "No problem, Juliusz, as it's you".

There are many other examples that I could give of how courtesies have been repaid many times over simply by always seeking to embrace the principles of spirituality in the workplace that I have outlined above. The intention is never to seek to create a bargaining position, it is just right and it is much more fun getting on with people than not!

How to Negotiate

Aggression is a "tactic" that has been (and is) used from time to time by other professionals in meetings, and negotiations. Some clients seem to relish this way of conducting business, and this is no doubt the case in other professions and industries.

My answer is quite simply to remain calm, remain patient, courteous and respectful, and to bide my time to deal with the matter, or point. My clients retain me to produce the deal that works for them, and this is the paramount objective, and one that I always deliver on, but in a way that embraces spiritual ethics.

I remember the time that I was involved in negotiations acting for a major property developer assembling a site for an office development, there being two sellers. One of the sellers was a major telecommunications company, the other an industrial conglomerate. A meeting was held at the offices of the solicitors to the telecommunications company, attended by all the parties and the respective lawyers and property advisers. The lead lawyer acting for one of the sellers (a recently promoted junior partner in a major City of London firm) was conducting the meeting in a very aggressive manner, seeking to belittle the points that my client was making in an effort (it seemed) to impress his client, and being not particularly pleasant in the way this was being done. I remained very calm, and just answered the points in a quiet and considered manner, and kept on quietly raising the issues that were important to my client.

A few hours into the meeting the various parties and their respective advisers broke out into separate meeting rooms to assess where the transaction had got to, and to reflect on the points that remained outstanding and problematical. The managing director of my client was there as was his junior development manager (who had not been at a meeting with me before). During that break out meeting the junior development manager asked me "Juliusz, why aren't you in there knocking him down and sorting him out?". The managing director smiled knowingly, and I replied, "Let's just see how we get on when we resume"

We continued the main meeting, and as before, the aggressive stance continued. After a little while the aggressive lawyer contradicted a statement that had previously been made by his client on a problematic point.

I quietly asked the other lawyer whether what he had just said reflected his instructions as his statement contradicted a point that his client had previously made. In further discussion between the other lawyer and his client it became clear that a point had been aggressively argued without instructions, and contrary to his clients requirements.

Now an aggressive lawyer became a humble lawyer. All of the points that were important to my clients were agreed speedily, and the meeting ended.

I went for a drink with the managing director and junior development manager from my client. It was interesting to hear the junior development manager say to me that he had been fascinated to see how such a first class result had been obtained through such a calm approach, with the only foil to aggression having been patience, calm, and waiting for the right opportunity to deal with the matter.

I believe that the right way to further my clients' interests, and to obtain the right deal for them, is always to deal with people on the other side of transactions (and my own client) in a proper and respectful manner, and to deal with the paperwork promptly, and when producing documentation to present a properly prepared package of documents so as to reduce the negotiating time.

Some time ago I was acting for a Japanese diagnostic centre taking a leasehold interest in a property in central London for medical clinical purposes. The transaction was fairly complex owing to the leasehold provisions, and the planning position relating to the property. The landlord was represented by a firm of solicitors based in the West End of London. My instructing officer was a Japanese gentleman who did not have a brilliant command of English, assisted by a surveyor from one of the major London firms of surveyors.

The landlord's solicitor tried what I would call every trick in the book to gain an unfair advantage in all of the legal documents, which as I say were fairly complex to begin with owing to the actual issues that we needed to deal with. Every time I thought that we had agreed a point, the documentation was further amended to reflect another point that was not agreed, and so it went on, and on. Finally, the documentation was agreed, and the transaction was completed, much to my client's relief. Understandably the English property system was a complete mystery to him, not helped by difficult lawyers!

So, the deal had been completed.

A few weeks after completion, I received a telephone call from the landlord's solicitor. "Juliusz, I omitted to provide for this particular clause in the lease and my client has spotted this. Can we enter into a deed of variation please, because otherwise my client as the landlord will not have an institutionally acceptable investment"?

My client's surveyor thought that it was tough luck, and that they should have to live with their error after having been so difficult. My client did not mind what we did, as he left these sorts of decisions to me, as from our perspective the point was not significant to my client as the tenant. On this basis I advised my client to agree to the variation, and we completed this.

I take the view that there is no point in compounding difficulties when we all need to move on. It is possible for all professionals to make errors, and I have always taken the view that if it is possible to rectify an error that is not inconsistent with my client's interests then it is best to do so.

It will be clear to all that the likelihood of assistance in what may be difficult circumstances is much more likely to be forthcoming when one has been co-operative throughout a transaction. Also, as stated before, the world is a small place, and people that we deal with pop up time and time again. It is not a good start to a transaction if you have fallen out with your opposite number previously!

Workplace Bullying

I have worked in various environments that have had the office "corporate" bully, and/or partners or bosses that have sought to exercise control through fear, anger or rage. I have witnessed members of staff being subjected to (what I consider to be) unacceptable behaviour, and which I will not tolerate.

Where witnessing such behaviour towards others I have either taken the matter up with the relevant person, and / or raised it with the human resources team or the senior partner, depending on the relevant structure in the firm. All firms should have a mechanism to deal with such matters. The difficulty often is that the "corporate bully" is the person who either generates significant business or fees, or holds a position of power. It can therefore be difficult to challenge the particular person. This can be due to fear, or because there is concern that the relevant person may leave and take all their clients and work away, leaving reduced profits and turnover.

Staff too are often afraid to raise issues for fear of reprisal, even though this should never be the case. Sometimes, staff will even deny that particular events have taken place through fear, thereby perpetuating a problem. If nobody speaks out, no action can be taken.

We need to remember that everybody has responsibility for their own actions, and nothing can be done about difficult situations unless people speak out in truth.

Where bullying tactics or aggression have been directed at me, I have stayed very calm, remained patient, and waited quietly, whilst maintaining direct eye contact. This is a very powerful response (some may say non-response), which has fielded a variety of reactions, ranging from absolute fury and rage exploding, to the aggressor becoming calm and being able to see the nature of their behaviour.

Whilst I may not always have been liked by the office "corporate bully" I have always held their respect, and have been able to say things to them that no other person would or could. Some of the things that I have said to my former partners, either individually or at partners' meetings have entered into the firm's folklore. I remember the time that there had been a very difficult period between a head of department and the staff as the head of department had been "bullying" junior staff for some time. After a protracted review, the senior partner and the head of department agreed on a way forward that meant that the head of department retained their position, but another partner was jointly elected as head. In subsequent discussion the head of department told me that he had been reflecting on things and had decided that he had changed as he could not continue happily working in the way that he had been. I asked him if he had "decided to change due to a spiritual shift in approach or because he needed to save his skin and position in the firm". On another occasion where I could not accept the corporate bullying tactics of a senior colleague I said that I refused to acknowledge their authority and that I would proceed on my own terms.

The above examples would not on the whole be appropriate for individuals to employ to deal with a bullying situation. The key way of dealing with these things is to remember that corporate bullies will usually behave in a bullying manner to those that they feel are unable to answer back. The important things to do are to keep a written log of all things said and done (with time, date and place), if things are done in front of others to have witnesses to events, to keep calm and not react, to tell others that you can trust, to tell the human resources manager. Always remember that none of these things are about you – they stem from the internal inadequacies of the corporate bully.

How to Be Happy at Work

It is helpful to remember that you are a unique, wonderful being, that is striving for understanding and happiness, and that the only moment that exists is now. Happiness is important for now, not tomorrow, not yesterday, now. That means that when you are at work, happiness needs to be with you at work.

To be content with every moment, and to live in the now, is the aim. To do this you need to begin with loving yourself, accepting yourself for what you are, recognising the unique and beautiful you. This can be so difficult at this time in this consumer society in which we live, but love yourself, and love will come to you, love yourself and it will be easier to take pleasure in all the tasks that you undertake, love yourself and it will not be easy for others to disturb your balance or your peace.

Whilst working towards acceptance of yourself, and love, take steps that make you feel good. Walk in the park, go swimming, go to the gym, the cinema, have lunch with friends, make love, whatever you want to do that makes you feel vibrant and alive, in balance with everything else whilst remaining sensitive to others and their needs. Do the things that are right for you, speak your truth with honesty and compassion, have fun, laugh, dance. Okay, you can't do all of these things at work, but you can be honest, compassionate and sensitive and speak your truth, you can share and laugh to the extent that others will join with you in your workplace.

All things have to start somewhere, from someone. If you wish to see changes, start with yourself! There is no better, or other place to start. If enough of us start with ourselves, there could be wholesale changes for the better. If everyone in your workplace started with themselves, what power would that wield, what changes could be made!

Changing Negative Patterns

As stated above, if we hold negative views about ourselves, and do not focus on what we wish to be, or achieve, and/or we hold onto behavioural patterns that may have formed over many years, the reality that we create for ourselves may be one that does not hold the best for us in this life or allow us to achieve our full potential, whatever that may be, and however it may manifest.

The first thing that is helpful to do is to look hard at what you do, how you behave, what is important to you, what you would wish to do, whether there are areas of your life that you wish to adapt or change, whether you feel that you have stagnated and would like to move forward in life, whether you have got stuck in a particular place and are finding it difficult to move out of it.

All process of change begins with the acceptance of what is, no matter how difficult it may be to do this. Without acceptance you cannot seek to change behavioural patterns, thought processes, attitudes, or reactions. If you deny parts of how you are, there cannot be any room for change, as you are effectively blocking that possibility.

This process can be a very difficult one as it can open up all sorts of emotions and traumas that have been deeply buried, anger that has been repressed, fears that have not been faced, personal issues that may have been hidden. The emotional floodgates can be opened and it may be that you will need help from family, friends, a partner, a counsellor, a healer, your higher self, your faith, to see you through this process.

Then decide what change you would like to bring about in your life.

Focus then on the aspect, or aspects that you wish to create and manifest in your life. Think it, breathe it, write it down and put it under your pillow, send the thoughts and the energy into the universe, feel that it is with you now. Structure a saying around the aspect along the lines "I am ---------- in my life right now", and repeat this to yourself or aloud seven times at a time, three times a day. Take these words deep into your being. Allow them to permeate all aspects of you. Send these words out to the universe, let it hear the energy with which it is sent, heartfelt, with truth and belief.

Be true to yourself, and others, and allow the truth to be with you.

The Illusion of Separation

It is important to remember that work is not a separate part of life, it is not a separate you that goes to work. It is the same you that is at work as is at home, or in the gym, it's just that you may feel very different about being in the workplace to elsewhere.

The point here is that people will wear what mask they feel is most appropriate in any given situation, whether this be work, socially, as a father or mother, as a lover.

There is no conflict in being what you are at any time, although one needs to be sensitive, compassionate and aware as to others and all of life. When you do things that are in line with love and truth, in a compassionate manner, with honesty and integrity, nothing can go wrong. That is not to say that what you may say, or the actions you carry out, may be liked by another. In fact those that speak the greatest truth and who have shown the greatest integrity have throughout history been the ones that have been the most persecuted. However it is not the purpose of life necessarily to be liked by another, the purpose is to be what you are, in accordance with your truth, to remember who and what you are.

There is no actual separation between the individual at work and the individual at home, or the individual with work colleagues or the individual with friends. The difference in attitude and behaviour in these different situations is largely due to how we feel we should behave largely as a result of our conditioning and upbringing.

You choose which of those aspects you wish to engage in at any time, such choices being made for a whole variety of reasons.

The bottom line though is that this is you. You are all things at all times. Which aspects of your being that you choose to engage in and show is a constantly evolving process changing from day to day, week to week, month to month and year to year. It is likely that the being that you choose to show at age 20 will be different to that at age 40.

Work is not a separate place of life, it is not a separate and different you that goes to the office, shop, factory or other place of work. When you go to work your spirituality goes with you, your healing processes are with you, the love that you may have with another is still present with you, and yet you go about doing your job.

So why is it that for many the workplace is seen as a necessary unhappiness that they have to undergo for five or six days in every week? Why is it that so many feel awful on Monday, but good on Friday as it is then nearly the weekend? Why are people saying during the week that they cannot wait for the weekend? Why do some live for their holidays (a few weeks in each year)? Why are people wishing so much of their lives away, instead of living in the love and joy that life should be?

As discussed elsewhere in this book, I believe that this comes down to people not being who they truly are in the workplace, that spiritual principles are not engaged in the workplace, that people are not encouraged to be what they truly are, to achieve their full potential both personally and professionally (the two go together).

Let Go of Attachment to Outcome

If we are not attached to the outcome of the task, it is more likely that the outcome will be one that is right, that will take us forward or be in accordance with what we wish for. By concentrating on the task in hand, by being in the present, in the now, and doing the best we can in carrying out the particular task the outcome of the task will be assured, the right result will be the outcome. If we concentrate on the outcome, how is the task going to have full concentration?

How often have you worried over what is going to happen at some future date about something that has not come to pass? How often have you rehearsed in your mind how people may react to things that you are planning to say or do, only to find that the response is completely different from that you have envisaged?

If, in all that you do, you do your best in the now, from the place of truth, how can things be other than right for you, how can things not follow your truth?

Be true to yourself at all times.

Honesty

Truth is just that, truth. Anything that is in accordance with the truth, in line with divine or natural law is immutable, absolute, and cannot be anything other.

If we are in line with absolute truth in accordance with divine or natural law we are talking about something that is outside of our normal physical senses. We are talking here about knowing, understanding, about how we live our lives on a personal basis, about being in tune with all that is around us, about living our lives in accordance with spiritual principles.

We need to be honest, to speak of things from a place of truth, compassionately and sensitively, we need to embrace this way of being at all times. We all need to be honest, truthful compassionate and sensitive.

What we perceive through our physical senses will be personal to us, as will the way in which this information is processed within our beings. Universal truth though is absolute, and applies to all beings absolutely. Seeking to live in accordance with this truth is what brings peace, understanding and contentment.

Live in your place of absolute truth.

Learn to be Happy

The above line was the heading of a piece written by John Elliott in The Sunday Times (7 January 2007). The first paragraph of this article read: "People who take the time to chat over the fence to their neighbours, ... and care about endangered species tend to be happier, according to Tony Blair's 'department for happiness'".

It appears that the Whitehall Wellbeing Working Group, a committee of civil servants, has been charged with finding out how ministers can make citizens more cheerful.

I have absolutely no doubt that those who talk to their neighbours (to others) will be happy people.

The aspect of communication is one that appears over and over again in this book as applying to business, as it does to relationships, shopping, friendship, family, education and every aspect of human life.

Caring about endangered species is an expression of compassion, and so people who have engaged in compassion are on a spiritual journey, and by (my) definition, will be happier.

It seems quite bizarre that the Government is seeking to make citizens happier when the answer to happiness lies within every individual. Happiness at a deep and sustainable personal level can never be provided by an outside source, although clearly aspects of outside life may influence how you feel, how you may respond to factors in your life. Music may be uplifting for some, others may be inspired by art, or theatre, or the attention of a loved one, or by sitting on a beach watching the sun go down, or sitting in a monastery in silence. Whatever the position may be, no matter how uplifting each and any of these aspects may be, at some point or another it or they will fade, and you will be back with yourself. It is that self, your self, that needs to be happy, only your self can achieve that constant state of contentment, only you can do this.

I am all for the promotion of happiness through whatever means, but I consider that this starts with every individual, you and me. If every individual embraces the principles of spirituality in his or her daily life, if everyone seeks to accept themselves and love themselves as they are, if every individual treats everyone at work in accordance with these principles, then how could work not be a brilliant place to be, an enjoyable place, supportive and nurturing, enabling you to make your living in a harmonious way whilst you continue on your personal journey through life?

From the above it can be seen that communication in the workplace from the place of honesty, integrity and compassion, and where there is social contact, may well increase individual happiness.

This also highlights the importance of a sensible work life balance for individuals to enable everyone to have such social contact that may be needed to enhance individual happiness.

Appoint a Director of Fun (yes, really!!)

In a previous firm, at a particularly difficult meeting where morale was at an all time low, I remember sitting there and suggesting that we appoint a director of fun, and that we should dedicate one afternoon a month to fun activities in the workplace. The silence that greeted this was stunning in its loudness. Nobody spoke, nobody could believe that I had just raised this as a serious suggestion; nobody thought that I was being serious.

I recall too how at one meeting where we were discussing morale issues in the department and I was talking in terms of motivation, respect, encouragement, acknowledging contributions, etc, the head of department said to me *"Juliusz, I am running a business here, you want to be some sort of corporate communist".*

The suggestion that the firm appoint a director of fun was my way of seeking to get a point across, of seeking to get some attention and focus onto things that had gone awry, where staff were not happy. I think that there should be fun at work, people should laugh and smile, there should be banter and ideas flowing freely, and this was my way of seeking to get to this place. What a difference would have been made to the workplace if a Director of Fun had been appointed!

There are businesses where the boss will go out and buy ice creams for the staff, where all are valued, where people engage with one another from the basis of respect and courtesy and share time together. These are some of the businesses where there is very low staff turnover, where there are seldom any vacancies, where people enjoy going into work and it almost becomes at one with their social lives. This is how it should be, work is not an enemy, it is part of what you do.

What would you look to do in your workplace to make it fun?

Love Your Client

At a partners' meeting in my current firm we were focusing upon business development activities, and methods of growing the business to achieve our vision. We were discussing, in particular, what is important to clients, and how to keep clients happy.

The normal aspects of client care were discussed and noted, things like quality of service, reasonable fees, keeping clients informed (communication again!), the right people doing the job, etc.

I piped up *"love your client"* Not a murmur, this was noted down as part of the client care strategy.

Just as we need to love ourselves to achieve happiness and contentment, so we need to see others in such a way. This is not confined to our personal relationships with our partner, family and friends, but to all people who we may meet, who we have dealings with. This will therefore include clients and customers, work colleagues, the bus driver, supermarket checkout people, everyone.

I am not talking about hugging everyone that we meet or talk to, or about seeking to be intimate with them, or about seeking to discuss what may be personal issues, or even seeking necessarily to like them (although you could try to find something to like about them even if it is only one thing!). I am again talking about employing spiritual principles in our dealings with everyone, and treating everyone with respect, sensitivity and compassion, and listening to what is being said and being aware. If we can look to find just one trait in a person that we can like, admire or respect on a personal level, that could make all the difference in how we interact with that person.

One of the issues that is often reported where there are failings as between clients and service providers is that "we were not told", or "I didn't understand that would happen"

Keep Calm

The ability to keep calm is something that has grown as my spiritual awareness has grown, as my knowing and understanding has increased, as I have come to accept myself for what I am. Knowing what you are, and doing the best that you can in the now, means that you can do no more. To worry perpetuates a cycle of exactly that, worry. It does not achieve the objective, or make anything better. It is more productive to turn the energy spent in worrying to sending thoughts of love and betterment to the situation or person in question and which of itself will then help to ease the particular situation. Remember all things follow thought.

As mentioned before we are mind, body and spirit, and so in addition to feeding the soul with spiritual awareness, we need to feed the mind and body. I have always sought to keep myself in good physical shape with a combination, over the years, of martial arts, running and swimming.

Diet is important, as is drinking plenty of water – as all good nutritionists and nutrition books will tell you. Mind wise, I have always taken an interest in many things, tried new languages, new courses, and (of course) meditation which not only feeds the mind, but also the soul. Sleep is restorative, and having adequate sleep is important. What is taken into the body by way of substances, will inevitably affect physical, emotional and mental functions, and (by way of example) alcohol is toxic to the body. I am not suggesting that you should not drink any alcohol, but moderation must be the watchword.

Afraid of Change?

People often find it difficult to seek to work, or be, outside of their comfort zones, whether in personal or work situations. There are relatively few people beyond their mid forties who relish the excitement of new challenges, new ways of tackling things, having to learn new methods.

Fear too of being faced with having to examine oneself, of having to look at one's own behaviour, way of being, and approach to work and or life. Fear of looking in the mirror and being left to see who and what one really is as opposed to how one seeks to portray oneself.

Fear of losing one's position, one's job, not being able to cope with demands made, or being able to complete the task when required.

Fear that by embracing change all will be lost, one will not be in control, others will take precedence.

Fear is a very non productive and negative emotion that holds many people back, that prevents people from seeking to fulfil their potential. It holds individuals back, and can also hold back whole groups of people either through collective fear, or because others follow the lead of one or more individuals who are stuck in this place.

Within the business environment fear can be catastrophic to motivation where fear is prevalent within the management as stagnation will be the end result. No change can be made, new clients will not be attracted, there will be limited (if any) openings for promotion, aggression and or bullying may occur.

Life, as a process, is about constant change, about learning, developing, moving and adapting. Human nature is intended to embrace change as and when it is right to do so for any individual, regardless of age. Not to do so is to arrest the natural process of development that all are inherently capable of, and this leads to stresses within the body that will reflect in negative behavioural patterns and/or illness.

PART FOUR: MEDITATIONS FOR DEALING WITH STRESS

Part Four: Meditations for Dealing with Stress

A Walking Meditation

As you approach your office, factory, shop where you work, slow your pace of walking.

Feel yourself become calmer, take a few deep breaths, notice the green of the leaves on the trees, the green of the grass, the green of any foliage in plant plots or tubs. Breathe in this colour green.

Remember that you were born with and already have all of the tools that are necessary for every situation that you might find yourself in, to deal happily with every person that you meet, to deal with every challenge that you might face.

Remember too that nothing that is presented to you is too difficult for you to manage, to deal with, and once dealt with you have the wealth of additional skills and knowledge.

As you come closer to your place of work, breathe in the colour pink, let this colour envelope you, surround you, be within you, the colour of love. Feel this colour, this love, flowing through you.

See your workplace, and all within it, placed in a pink bubble of light. See the corridors, the offices, all places in the workplace, filled with the colour pink. See your bosses, your work colleagues, surrounded with the colour pink. See this colour infusing the fabric of all parts of the building where you work, being absorbed by all who work within it.

Be aware that with this colour all aggression is dissolved, harmony is created and all possibilities are created.

Walk into the place of your work, feeling this harmony, feeling this peace.

Walk peace, be peace, respond to others with peace. Feel the peace within the workplace.

Work with calm, love and focus.

On the tube

See this time as your personal time for reflection and contemplation. Imagine that you are walking in the mountains.

The sky is blue, low golden sun, snow on the mountain tops.

As you walk along the path you look into the cool blue lakes to the right of the path that you are walking along. The birds are singing in the sky, flying high above the earth, free. The golden rays of the sun are warming your body.

You feel at peace, as if everything is right with you, and right with life.

As you walk along you become aware of a rock that is shaped like a bench, just ahead of you. You walk to this rock and sit down. You breathe the clear fresh air deep into your lungs, filling the whole of your chest with this wondrous vibrant energy. The golden sun's rays are playing over you, warming you, the golden colour of the sun being absorbed within you.

You stop to notice how the golden colour feels within your body, warming, expanding your consciousness, flowing through and around your body, changing your level of understanding. You look at the cool blue colour of the lake, the beautiful blue of the sky, and you breathe in the colour of the water, of the sky.

As you breathe this colour deep into your being you feel yourself expand yet more, your consciousness touching all that there is, you feel the lines of communication opening, you begin to understand life itself.

You look at the white of the snow on the mountains, see the perfect form of the snowflake, recognise the perfection of life itself. As you breathe in the colour of the snow, your consciousness expands yet further to take in the whole of life as we can know it, becoming one with life itself.

You are at your tube stop.

A mantra for you to try on a daily basis

As you sit quietly, or are walking along, or sitting on a tube, train or bus, say the following either to yourself (or if you are alone) out loud:

I am the love that shines from my soul

I am the light that gives me life

I am the best that I am

I am beautiful in my being

I am unique in my seeing

I am the whisper in the breeze

I am the blossoms on the trees

I am the sunset in the sky

I am the moon that shines at night

I am the result of my creation

I am at peace with all there is

I am love

I am.

A healing saying

When sitting quietly by yourself say the following aloud, or to yourself if others are around you:

I am the love that I am,

you are the love that you are,

together we are the love that we are,

the love that we are is the love that I am,

the love that I am is the love that you are,

the love that you are is the love that I am,

I am love.

A relaxation meditation (Try it at lunchtime)

Find yourself somewhere quiet to sit.

Close your eyes, place your feet flat on the floor, and sit with your back nice and straight.

Feel your body relaxing, your muscles unlocking, the tensions from your body leaving.

Breathe gently and deeply, feeling your stomach rise and fall with the in and out breaths.

Hold your hands in your lap, palms facing upwards. Feel your body becoming warmer, your hands becoming warmer.

Notice as your body begins to feel as if it is gently held in a soft blanket of white cotton wool, warm, gentle to the touch, safe, secure. Breathe deeply, counting your in breaths, your out breaths, noticing your stomach rise and fall with each one.

On your next in breath, follow the flow of life giving air as it enters your nostrils, passes down into your lungs, is absorbed by your blood and taken round your body. Feel the vitality of this oxygen as it circulates around your being. Feel the life force tingling within you, reaching every part of you.

Slowly and gently raise your hands upwards, palms facing up, to a level that is comfortable for you, roughly in line with the bottom of your rib cage.

Hold that position as you take some more gentle deep breaths.

Feeling safe, secure and loved cocooned in this warm, gentle blanket of cotton wool, become aware of a globe of light descending into the palms of your hands, slowing and stopping gently as it touches your hands. Feel the lightness of this globe, feel the coolness of its touch against the skin of your palms.

As you hold the globe become aware of the rays of light that are emanating from the centre of it, brilliant white light, leaving in all directions. You feel the brilliance of this light as it enters your hands, your stomach, your heart, you feel loved, safe, warm.

The light moves gently, powerfully, lovingly through, within and around all parts of your being. You feel the light coursing through you, you notice parts of you moving, shifting, pains leaving, emotions settling.

You feel complete, at peace.

As you hold the globe, you notice that the white light has changed form, and is radiating brilliant red, orange, yellow, green, blue, magenta and violet light.

All of these colours are now washing over, through and within you, pulsing, warm, vibrant.

You breathe deeply, feeling your breath absorbing the beauty of the colours.

As you sit quietly you notice that the light from the globe is white again, cool, but warming brilliant white. You are aware that the globe is now going to leave you.

Gently the globe rises from your hands, and ascends, returning to where it has come from, the place of all wisdom, knowledge and love. The globe has shared this wisdom, knowledge and love with you, shared the beauty of all that there is.

You lower your hands back to your lap, breathe in and out, move your hands and your feet, and return your awareness to where you are sitting, to the room that you are in, to the present. You have a glass of water.

You remember the love that has been shared with you. You are aware of feeling lighter, more at peace, you are aware that you are clearer and ready to move forward in the way that is right for you, to what and where you wish to be.

Breathing for calm and energy (Anytime)

Stop.

Stand still with your feet shoulder width apart.

Bend your knees slightly.

Relax your shoulders, gently move your shoulders, your head, your neck.

Be still.

Place your hands straight down by your sides, and focus on your breath.

Breathe deeply, slowly, filling the whole of your lungs, and exhale all of the air, slowly.

As you breathe in, deeply, slowly, raise your hands and arms, keeping them straight, until your hands meet above your head.

From the top of your head, as you breathe out fully and slowly, move your hands down in an oval shape in front of you, out in front of your shoulders, back towards your middle as you bring your hands together.

Turn your hands over so that the palms are facing upwards, ends of fingers touching, and slowly keeping your hands in that position raise your hands slowly, taking a deep breath as you do so, raising your hands to a place in front of your forehead.

When your hands have stopped moving upwards, turn your hands over so that the palms face downwards, ends of fingers together, and slowly, as you breathe out slowly, bring your hands down to your waist.

Again, turn your hands so that your palms face upwards, ends of fingers touching, breathe in deeply and slowly, and as you do so, move your hands slowly up to your throat.

Turn them over again, and breathing out all of the air move them back down to your waist.

Return your hands to your sides, arms straight.

Repeat the above breathing exercise twice (three times in all), remembering to breathe in very deeply and slowly on the in breath, and exhaling fully on the out breath.

When you have completed the exercise three times, instead of bringing your hands back to your sides, bring your hands to a prayer position in front of your chest.

Breathe deeply, slowly, exhale deeply, and slowly.

Repeat the exercise whenever you feel stressed, or tired, or in need of a boost of energy.

A meditation for complete body relaxation (good at the end of the day)

At a quiet time, in a quiet room, lie down comfortably, close your eyes. Still your mind.

Breathe in deeply, exhale, relax.

Take your mind to your feet, feel your toes, your feet relax, feel the tension leaving through the heels.

Move your attention to your calf muscles. Feel the muscles relax, soften, letting go of all the tension, the stresses and strains.

Slowly move your attention to your knees, feel them relax, without strain.

Then move your attention to your thighs, feeling them pressing into the surface, free of tension, soft, yielding.

Move your attention to your hips, feel them loosen, without weight, light.

Slowly move your attention to the small of your back, to your middle back, your upper back, spine and shoulders, your arms and hands and fingers.

Feel the whole of your back sigh with relief as all of the stresses and strains move away, feel your back supple, soft, relaxed.

Move your attention to your neck, your head, the crown of your head.

Feel all tension drain away, leaving you and your mind clear, stress free, calm.

Lie still, your body heavy with relaxation, feel yourself filled
with calm, with peace, with love. Feel the support of the earth
beneath you, the energy of the earth surrounding you and
infusing you. Feel the spiritual energy of love connecting to you,
flowing, embracing you.

Lie still, allow the earth's clearing, cleansing energy, and the love
to flow over, around and within you. Feel every muscle, every
organ, every cell, loved, cleansed, healed, relaxed. Lie still in this
place of calm, relaxed, for as long as you wish.

When you are ready, become aware of where you are, feel the earth
beneath you, the surface on which you are lying, become aware
of your body, your head, neck, back, arms, hands, fingers, hips,
upper legs, knees, lower legs, feet, toes Move each and every part
of your being. Open your eyes, return to your place of being.

PART FIVE: CONCLUSION

Part Five: Conclusion

And finally

Spirituality in the workplace is a hugely important issue. I have witnessed many injustices at work, bullying from corporate bullies, people not stopping to think how their actions affect others. I have also seen how positive influences in the workplace can enhance peoples lives. If one workplace is enhanced by an employer reading this book and reflecting on the ideas and thoughts here, I will consider that a significant outcome. For me, this is one of the ultimate challenges facing each and every one of us as we struggle in what is often a topsy turvy world. If we can have a greater degree of happiness in the place where we spend so much of our waking time it must follow that there will be a greater feeling of fulfilment within all of us at all times.

When we stop to think about the principles of spirituality in the workplace we can see that they make absolute sense. We can also see how much benefit would be brought not only to the individuals within the business, but to the business itself, its core objectives. The core message is fairly simple.

Something being simple of itself does not mean that people are aware of it, or embrace those practices. It is often the case that we become aware of things when we read about them, when we discuss things, when we see films, watch television, listen to the radio. We learn as we go through life, we have experiences, and remember those experiences. As the situation, or a similar one, arises in the future we recall how we resolved the last one and employ the methods then learnt.

This can mean that not only do we employ helpful and positive ways of dealing with things. It can also mean that we have learnt to reinforce ways of doing things, or behavioural patterns, that may not be terribly helpful, or right as we go through life and develop.

In other words, all of the tools that you need for life are within you, all the wisdom and knowledge you need are available to you already, but you need to remember all of this through your spiritual journey into awareness of life and understanding. This understanding does come, and the reason that it does is so beautifully simple.

Many people will seek to shroud understanding and knowledge in mystery. A new way of spiritual understanding, a new and better way of healing, a more direct method of connection, and so it goes on. Some of these practices and ways are no doubt effective and helpful, but it all comes down to love.

Work towards remembering who you are, the perfect, unique and beautiful you. You are mind, body and soul, you are more than your physical body. You create your reality in every single moment of every day. You have the potential to be whatever you wish to be, to have happiness, love, joy and wealth in abundance. You are perfect just as all others are perfect. Look to see the beauty in everyone, at all places and at all times. This applies to the you at work just as it does to the you at all other times.

Whether you are an employer or an employee, the aim of business is to make a profit. By harnessing the talent of all in a respectful way, and in accordance with the principles contained in this book, the lives of all individuals in the workplace will be enhanced, wellbeing will be increased, and productivity and profit will increase.

This is not something that should be legislated for by the Government. This is something that we should all be working towards now.

I wish each and everyone health, happiness and love in the workplace, and at all times.

Appendix : Information

My own websites:
www.juliuszw.com
and/or
www.healingheart.org.uk

Other places to find out more about healing:
NFSH
Manor Farm Studio
Church Street
Sunbury on Thames
Middlesex
TW16 6RG
Tel + 44 (0) 1932 783164
www.nfsh.org.uk

UK Reiki Federation
(a reiki umbrella organisation with links to members)
PO Box 71,
Andover, SP11 9WQ
Telephone:
0870 850 2209
www.reikfed.co.uk

UK Healers
(a spiritual healing umbrella organisation with links to members)
www.ukhealers.info

About meditation:
Brahma Kumaris
www.bkwsu.org.uk

About healing with song and music:
Lou Beckerman
www.loubeckerman.com

Notes

Notes

Notes

Notes

Notes